DYNAMIC NUN
by Tac

Editor: Mike Lee
Graphic Design: Karen Massad

Art Production: Junko Sadjadpour
Ludovic Szvercsak
Sergio Onaga

Twelfth printing 2004

WARNING

This book is presented only as a means of preserving a unique aspect of the heritage of the martial arts. Neither Ohara Publications nor the author makes any representation, warranty or guarantee that the techniques described or illustrated in this book will be safe or effective in any self-defense situation or otherwise. You may be injured if you apply or train in the techniques illustrated in this book. To minimize the risk of training injury, nothing described or illustrated in this book should be undertaken without personal, expert instruction. In addition, it is essential that you consult a physician regarding whether or not to attempt anything described in this book. Federal, state or local law may prohibit the use or possession of any of the weapons described or illustrated in this book. Specific self-defense responses illustrated in this book may not be justified in any particular situation in view of all of the circumstances or under the applicable federal, state or local law. Neither Ohara Publications nor the author makes any representation or warranty regarding the legality or appropriateness of any weapon or technique mentioned in this book.

BLACK BELT BOOKS
A Division of **OHARA ⏹ PUBLICATIONS, INC.**
World Leader in Martial Arts Publications

Dedication

In deep appreciation for their countless contributions to the art and philosophy of karate, I dedicate this text to my grandmaster Chosin Chibana, my master Saguro Nakazato, and my students throughout the world.

Acknowledgement

I would like to thank four very fine martial artists: Sam Kuoha, James Lew, Teik Huat Ooi, and Richard Rebago, for their expert assistance in demonstrating the techniques in this book.

About the Author

Tadashi Yamashita was born in Japan in 1942, but he considers himself an Okinawan. His father died when he was three, and his mother, who never remarried (the older Japanese did not believe in remarriage) moved to Okinawa when Tadashi was eight years old. He lived in Okinawa until, at the age of 24, he came to the United States where he has since become a citizen.

Yamashita's experience of more than 27 years in martial arts began at the age of 11. The roughest kid in school, he not only picked fights with the other students, but with the teachers as well. This was brought to the attention of the PTA which realized it could not handle him.

One day, the PTA president, who was also a karate instructor, stopped by to pick up Tadashi after school. Always the warrior, Tadashi tried to fight him. The instructor slapped the rebellious youngster and dragged him off to the dojo where he was taught the elements of kicking, punching, and most important of all, discipline. Tadashi found his probation period very interesting. His destructiveness was channeled into a hidden talent. The young man had discovered an art form, a religion, and a way of life. Yamashita was awarded his black belt at the age of 16. In 1960, he captured the All-Okinawan Shorin-ryu Free Sparring Grand Champion title.

On Okinawa, in addition to practicing martial arts, he was also an outstanding baseball pitcher, and collected some 60 trophies for motorcycle racing.

When he came to the United States, he opened a karate school which he owned and operated for five years.

In 1968, he visited Japan and tested before his instructor, Sugura Nakazato, ninth-degree black belt. Also on the panel was the famous Chosin Chibana, tenth-degree black belt. Tadashi became the youngest seventh-degree black belt in Japan's history.

In 1972, in search of a fuller life, Tadashi moved to Southern California. At the Pro-Am Tournament in Los Angeles in 1973, the first of many tournaments in which he would demonstrate his talent, Yamashita brought 7,000 spectators to their feet for a standing ovation, and from then on, his reputation in the United States as a karate and weapons expert grew.

During the same year, Yamashita was featured on the television show *Thrillseekers* with Chuck Connors. After that program aired in Japan, Toei Productions starred him in his first motion picture, *The Karate*. This film was so well received that Toei used him in two more films, *The Blind Karate Man* and *Karate II*. Some American films in which Yamashita has appeared include Warner Bros.' *Enter the Dragon*, Cannon Films' *American Ninja*, and American Cinema Productions' *Octagon* with Chuck Norris.

Yamashita is one of the foremost karate and weapons expert in the United States today. He is the head instructor of Shorin-ryu in the United States, and the head instructor of American Karate Association.

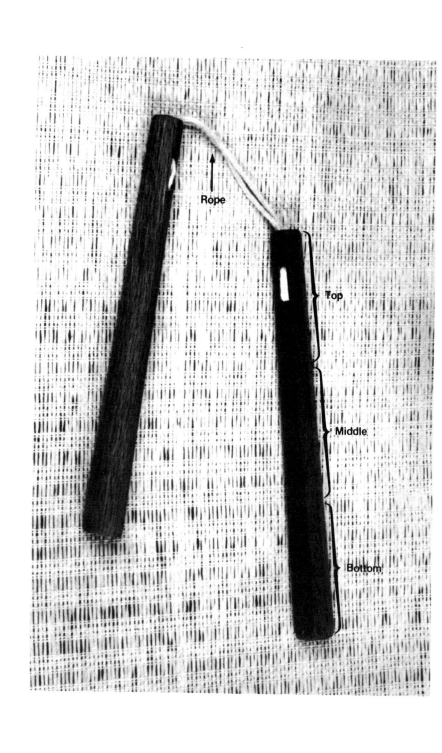

Anatomy of the Nunchaku

The traditional belief is that after countless hours of practice and hard work, your nunchaku will take on some of your spirit and character. When you begin to feel this way, that the weapon is becoming a part of you, you'll know that your skill is at the threshold of becoming real and viable.

Each of the nunchaku sections can be gripped in three places: the top, which is where the rope is connected, the middle, and the bottom; and each of these areas is a little more than the length of your fist, making the total length of each section about the same as the distance from your elbow to the middle of your hand, although this may also vary according to your preference.

The nunchaku sections are made of hardwood, and are connected together by rope, or in the case of those of less traditional construction, by chain. It is always wise to check both the wood for splinters and the connecting rope or chain to make sure all parts are sound and secure before every practice session.

Contents

Preparing for Practice

You should always warm up thoroughly before you begin practice. You'll find that you will make fewer mistakes, and that this will increase your confidence. Then you can build on the skills you already have. This is the natural way of learning and the best.

The worst kind of practice is that in which you make too many errors, in which the weapon becomes your enemy, and you develop bad habits due to incorrect technique and insecurity about the weapon. This is usually the case if you start out cold, ignore the basics, and overstep your skills too far.

This warm-up exercise is extremely simple. The truth is what specific things you do to warm up are really less important than your state of mind. This warm-up routine is enough to stretch your body properly but simple enough to allow you to relax and clear your mind.

1

Warm-Up Routine

With both sections together, (1) extend the nunchaku out at arms length and at shoulder height. (2) Raise it overhead, then (3) slowly lean your upper body to the left side, keeping your shoulders squared, and feeling the stretch in your right side. Next, (4) lean slowly to the right to stretch the left side in the same way. (5) Come back to an upright position, and lower the nunchaku to shoulder height. (6) Bend forward, keeping your knees straight, but not completely locked. Let the weight of your upper body bring your hands to the floor. Think of relaxing the muscles in your back and in the back of your legs. As these muscles relax, your upper body will sink

4

2

3

5

6

Continued

lower. (7) Come back to an upright position, and pivot to your left on the balls of both feet to establish a left side stance. As you do this, bring the nunchaku into an over-the-shoulder ready position on your right side. Exert dynamic tension. (8) Pivot back to your left on the balls of both feet to establish a right side stance, and repeat the over-the-shoulder ready position on the left side, exerting dynamic tension as before. (9) Straighten your legs as you swing forward to touch your left toes. (10) Swing to the right to touch your right toes. (11) Come back to an upright posture, and turn the nunchaku so the top points down, twisting your wrists outward. (12) With knees slightly flexed, point the nunchaku straight ahead, and reach. Push your shoulders forward to stretch your upper back muscles. (13) Fold the nunchaku and straighten your legs, ready to begin again. Repeat five times.

7

10

11

8

9

12

13

Drawing the Nunchaku

Okinawans, using the nunchaku as a self-defense weapon in the days when kobujutsu was the best insurance against coming to harm, often carried it hidden from sight. When enemies threatened, these men could draw their nunchaku into action without a moment's hesitation. This chapter demonstrates how to accomplish these kinds of draws.

Above all, when practicing these draws, be smooth. Keep your eyes on the opponent at all times, and when you draw, do it with the sense of urgency that a real confrontation would evoke. In practicing in this way, you'll notice immediately how it is possible to be extremely fast while keeping an inner calm. Remember this because it is an important feeling that will be of value to you as you progress.

Drawing from the Waist

(1) The nunchaku remains hidden under your clothing tucked in behind your belt. The top is pointing inward. Reach in and (2) draw. In one motion, use your other hand to (3) grip one of the sections, restraining it as you

begin to exert force on the other section, pushing it toward your target. Then, (4) release your restraining grip, and snap forward into your imaginary target, extending your whole arm into the forward strike.

Drawing from the Sleeve

(1) With the nunchaku tucked into the sleeve with the top pointing inward, grip the nunchaku by bending your wrist. (2) As you pull it out, extend your arm forward, and grip one section with your thumb and index finger while supporting the other with your other fingers. (3) When the nunchaku clears your sleeve, allow the bottom section to drop while maintaining your grip on the top section with your thumb and index finger. When the bottom section falls clear of your hand, grip the top section with your whole hand in a backhand grip. (4) To swing the free section, recoil the nunchaku over to the outside and swing to the inside, flipping your wrist to (5) strike with a sideward sweep.

Drawing from Behind

Begin with the nunchaku tucked in back under your belt, the top pointing down. (1) Grab both sections, and (2) draw from behind. One of the sections will be closer to your palm. (3) Secure your grip on this one, and allow the other one to fall free of your hand. From your right side, (4) swing the nunchaku forward, striking with the free section in a circular motion across the front of your body, and (5) catch with your left hand at your left hip.

2

4

5

REAR VIEW

Drawing from the Collar

(1) Start with the nunchaku tucked under your collar at the back of your neck, the top pointing down. (2) Draw by gripping only one of the sections. The other will be drawn out along with it, and will fall free. With the draw, the free section will be resting close to your face. It is necessary that your first

3

move pulls this free section away from your face. Your swing should go out in an arc away from your face, then around and (3) across the front of your body to execute the strike. (4) Catch with your right hand, and come to another ready position.

4

Developing
Lightning Dexterity

It isn't difficult for an attacker, given the privilege of making the first move, to jam a defender's technique. Faced with a situation that can't be handled in an orthodox way, the defender's weapon for that instant actually becomes a liability to him.

Though the nunchaku can overcome any attack, unless you are versatile with it, you're better off without it. These practice routines can develop your dexterity so that you can be flexible and spontaneous with the nunchaku, able to answer any situation.

Learn the movements so you can do them at full speed and focus. Then, use them as examples from which to develop your own practice routines, creating moves that make sense, but which force you to practice what you cannot do well.

This chapter is divided into three general categories, emphasizing skills which are common weaknesses among students at this level. They are: controlling the nunchaku after a fully focused strike; changing directions without recoiling off your body; and twirling the nunchaku. The advanced student, in addition to his formal training, must begin to instruct himself in his own way. These practice exercises provide a way of beginning that advanced level of learning.

Controlling the Nunchaku After a Fully Focused Strike

It is often said that the nunchaku can pose more of a threat to the unskilled user than to any opponent he may face, and that only traditional training can develop the skill to use it competently. Surely,

Control Exercise No. 1

The most common error in catching the nunchaku after a strike is letting it bounce out of the palm of your catching hand before closing your fingers around it. This results from stiffening your catching hand. It must be relaxed. The catching action has to be as if the force of the nunchaku is what causes the hand to collapse around it. (1) Hold the nun-

this is true in a way that can only be described as morally beautiful. Essential to the acquisition of skill is your ability to control your weapon, just as self-control is essential to traditional martial arts training.

chaku out at chest level. (2) Step into a forward stance, and turn one side of your body toward the target. (3) With your lead hand, snap the nunchaku forward with focus. (4) Allow it to complete its natural swing down and back toward you. Then, catch it quickly with your free hand, ready to strike again.

Control Exercise No. 2

(1) With the nunchaku at waist level, (2) step back with your left foot into a right forward stance, bringing the nunchaku into a front ready position. (3) Release your left hand grip, and simultaneously flip a forward strike with your right hand, (4) pulling back and catching the nunchaku once again in your left hand. (5) Pull back, and (6) thrust a strike with the

1

3

5

Continued

right section. (7) Twist your upper body to the right as you pull back the right section and bring the left section out to your left shoulder in a ready position. (8) Release your right hand grip, and flip a circular strike from your left shoulder across the front. Be sure, during the first instant of this strike, that you pull the nunchaku clear of your face before whipping it into the strike. Still, it should all be one motion. (9) Catch the strike in your right hand. (10) Pull back the nunchaku as you step up with your left foot squaring your feet with your shoulders, and (11) thrust a strike to the left side with the left section.

6

9

7

8

10

11

33

Control Exercise No. 3

(1) Begin in a right forward stance, holding the nunchaku in a front ready position. (2) Release your left hand grip and simultaneously flip a forward strike with your right hand. (3) Follow through, letting the nunchaku swing through a downward arc and back toward your body. (4) Catch it underhand with your left hand. (5) Turn the left section upright as you step forward with your left foot into a left forward stance, and (6&7) thrust a strike with the left section, leaning your body weight into the thrust for focus.

1

4

5

3

7

35

Control Exercise No. 4

Following through after a strike is another way of controlling the nunchaku. (1) Begin with the nunchaku at waist level in front of your body. (2) Pivot to your left on the balls of your feet into a left side stance, carrying the nunchaku over to your right side into an over-the-shoulder ready position on your right side. (4) Release your left hand grip, and (5) execute a downward strike with speed and focus. This strike should be focused at the head of your imaginary opponent. Follow through by (6) continuing the motion of your arm, slowing the nunchaku to a stop by the time your arm is fully extended at your side. Following through prevents the free section from going out of control.

1

4

3

6

Control Exercise No. 5

Controlling the nunchaku on the follow-through is most necessary when using two nunchaku since you have no way of catching them except under your arms. (1) With both nunchaku secured in ready positions under your arms, assume a forward stance facing your target. (2) Execute a right horizontal strike across the front, and control the nunchaku by (3) following through to the opposite side of your body. (4) Execute a left horizontal strike across the front, and control the nunchaku by once again (5) following through to the opposite side.

5

Control Exercise No. 6

This exercise contains a variety of swinging strikes. They require that you recover control quickly by following through on your swing even while you begin another strike with the other nunchaku. (1) In a forward stance with both nunchaku in ready positions under your arms, (2) strike directly forward with both nunchaku simultaneously. Both strikes are focused at the face of your imaginary opponent. Follow through on these striking motions, bringing the nunchaku out to the sides. (3) Execute a diagonal strike with the right nunchaku, and (4) follow through to the left hip. Then immediately (5) bring it off the left hip, and reverse directions to execute another diagonal strike upward. At the same time, execute a diagonal strike with the left nunchaku. (6) While the right nunchaku swings up to the right shoulder in a reverse diagonal strike, the left nunchaku swings down to the right hip in a diagonal strike of its own. Next, (7) execute a diagonal strike with the right nunchaku by (8) swinging it through an inside-out path, focusing at your opponent's right side, and pull back to the left hip. Then, (9) execute another inside-out diagonal strike with the left nunchaku, focusing at your opponent's left side.

Changing Directions Without Recoiling Off Your Body

The basic method of changing directions with the nunchaku is by recoiling it off part of your body, and then pulling it into its new direction. There is another way of changing directions which is faster; however, it requires more skill.

Although the free section will have a tendency to flip back toward your hand when you stop abruptly after a fully focused strike, if you keep a flexible wrist, you can whip the nunchaku into a new direction quickly without having the free section go out of control. Your wrist softens the abruptness by compensating, bending back, half way at the most, like a whip, then once some speed is gained toward the new direction, whips forward again into its natural attitude before focus.

Direction Change Exercise No. 1

(1) In a right forward stance with the nunchaku in a front ready position. (2) Release your left hand and flip a forward strike, (3) following through in a downward direction. (4) Flip the nunchaku quickly back upward over your right shoulder, and (5) catch it with your left hand on the right side in an over-the-shoulder ready position, but don't hold it there. Immediately release your right hand. As soon as your left hand catches

5

Continued

the nunchaku, release your right. (6) Swing a backhand horizontal strike across the front, and (7) follow through. (8) Snap the nunchaku out of the horizontal follow-through into an upward flip (9) over the left shoulder, and catch it with your right hand on your left side. (10) As soon as your right hand catches it, (11) release your left hand, and execute a downward block across the front.

Direction Change Exercise No. 2

(1) Holding the nunchaku at waist level, (2) pivot to the left on the balls of both feet into a left side stance, and (3) shift the nunchaku over to your right side into an over-the-shoulder ready position. (4) Pivot back to the left on the balls of both feet into a right side stance, and (5) release your right hand grip to (6) strike horizontally from right to left with your

1

4

Continued

left hand. (7) Flip the nunchaku upward from the horizontal follow-through. Your change of direction here must be crisp and clean. You must whip the nunchaku into its upward motion instantly with a flexible wrist. Then, (8) flip it over your left shoulder and catch it with your right hand in an over-the-shoulder position at your left side. (9) Pivot into a left side stance, and (10) release your left hand, (11) striking horizontally with your right hand. (12) Immediately come back in the opposite direction with another horizontal strike. Here again, your change of direction must be quick to prevent the free section from flipping out of control. (13) Catch it on your left hip with your left hand.

7

10

11

9

13

Direction Change Exercise No. 3

(1) Begin with the nunchaku at waist level, and from your horse stance, (2) pivot slightly to your left on the balls of both feet into a left side stance, and flip the nunchaku over your right shoulder, (3) catching it in an over-the-shoulder position with your left hand at your right side. (4&5) Release your right hand as soon as you catch it in your left, and execute a horizontal strike across the front, pivoting back to the right side simultaneously. (6) Snap it out of the horizontal follow-through into an over-the-shoulder catch with the right hand on your left side. (7) With both hands maintaining their grip on the nunchaku, bring it forward as you pivot back into a horse stance.

1

4

5

3

7

Direction Change Exercise No. 4

(1) Begin in a horse stance, nunchaku at the ready position in front of you. (2) Step back with your left foot, establishing a right forward stance, and snap a forward strike. (3) Catch it underhand with your left hand, (4) turn it upright, and (5) stepping forward with your left foot into a left forward stance, thrust a strike to the throat of your imaginary op-

1

3

2

4

5

Continued

ponent. (6) Maintaining hold with both hands, shift the nunchaku into an over-the-shoulder ready position at your right side. (7) Release your left hand grip, and execute a downward inside-out diagonal strike focused at your opponent's neck on his right side. (8) Change directions by snapping the nunchaku horizontally over to the left side of your body, (9) flipping it under your left arm, and catching it with your left hand in an over-the-shoulder ready position. (10) Release your right hand grip, and execute an inside-out downward diagonal strike focused at your opponent's neck on his left side.

6

8

7

9

10

Direction Change Exercise No. 5

(1) From a left forward stance with the nunchaku in a ready position in front, (2) step up with your right foot, and pivot to your right into a right stance, bringing the nunchaku into an over-the-shoulder ready position on the left side. (3) Execute a downward strike, and (4) snap the nunchaku back up, (5) catching it with your right hand. (6) Pivot on the balls of both feet into a left side stance while you shift the nunchaku into an over-the-shoulder ready position on your right

Continued

side. (7) Execute a downward strike, and (8) snap the nunchaku back up, flipping it over your right shoulder, and catching it with your left hand in an over-the-shoulder ready position on your right side. (9) Step back with your left foot, establishing a right forward stance as you bring the nunchaku into thrusting position. (10) Twist the rope around your right wrist, (11) bring it to the right side, and (12) execute a downward block with your right arm.

Direction Change Exercise No. 6

(1) Starting in a right forward stance with both nunchaku in ready positions under your arms, (2) snap both nunchaku to strike forward, focusing at the face of your imaginary opponent. (3) Flip both nunchaku through half circles on the outsides of your wrists, and finish the circles on the insides to (4) catch under your arms. (5) Bring the right nunchaku to an over-the-shoulder ready

1

3

2

4

5

Continued

6

position over the right shoulder, and (6) as you flip the left nunchaku toward the same position on the left shoulder, simultaneously (7&8) execute a downward strike with the right nunchaku. (9) Flip the right nunchaku back as you strike down with the left. (10) With the right nunchaku in an over-the-shoulder position and the left nunchaku down at your side, you're ready to begin another series of alternating strikes.

8

10

Twirling the Nunchaku

This aspect of nunchaku training is for developing an extra sharpness to your dexterity with the nunchaku. In most twirling techniques, using a plain baton can be of some aid in understanding the mechanical details involved in the movements. Though the nunchaku is actually easier to flip since it is flexible, the baton permits you to try the moves slowly while you're still learning.

Twirling Exercise No. 1

(1) With the nunchaku at chest level, (2) simultaneously release your left hand grip, and flip the nunchaku by twisting your right hand in a clockwise direction. (3) As the free section comes round to complete the circle, release your right hand grip and quickly snap your right hand back in a counterclockwise direction to catch the free section. (4) Continue the circular motion of the nunchaku by twisting your wrist again clockwise, and repeat by (5) releasing your right hand grip, snapping your right hand back counterclockwise, and catching the free section as it comes round to complete the circle.

4

5

Twirling Exercise No. 2

(1) Stand in a horse stance with the nunchaku in both hands, palms up. (2) Release your left hand and simultaneously flip your right hand counterclockwise so that the free section goes round in a circle. (3) As the free section comes over the top to complete the circle, and your right hand is turned almost completely around in a close to palm up position, release your right hand, and twist it back clockwise to catch the free section in a palm up position as it completes its circle. (4) Next, flip your right hand counterclockwise to a palm down position and catch the other section of the nunchaku in your left hand. (5) Repeat this movement with your left hand by releasing your right hand grip and flipping the free section through a clockwise circle. (6) As it comes over the top to complete the circle, release your left hand grip and (7) catch the free section. (8) Flip the nunchaku once more through a half circle and catch with your right hand. (9) Bring the nunchaku back to its original horizontal starting position.

Twirling Exercise No. 3

(1) From a right forward stance with the nunchaku at chest level in front of you, (2) twist the rope around your left wrist, and (3) thrust a strike to the throat of your imaginary opponent. (4) Bring the nunchaku into an over-the-shoulder ready position on your right side. (5&6) Execute a downward strike as you simultaneously step up with your left

5

Continued

foot and pivot on the balls of both feet into a left side stance. (7) Pivot on both feet into a right side stance as you extend your left arm forward. (8) From underneath, swing the nunchaku up to your extended left wrist, and, letting go, (9) allow it to flip completely free around your left wrist. It will naturally fall off as it completes one rotation. (10) Catch it by extending your right wrist, and allow-

10

Continued

11

ing the nunchaku to fall across the top. (11) Twist your right hand counterclockwise, and grasp the outer section of the nunchaku. (12&13) Pivot into a left side stance, and swing the nunchaku down and diagonally to the left side, then upward on the left to complete half a figure eight. (14&15) Then, pivot back into a right side stance and come over the top then down diagonally to the right side to complete the second half of the figure eight. (16) Snap the free section under toward you, and catch it with your left hand to come back to a ready position in a right forward stance.

14

2

13

5

16

Twirling Exercise No. 4

(1) Begin in a left side stance with the nunchaku in your right hand. (2) Shift your weight to your right leg, and lift your left knee up to waist level. Swing the nunchaku under your left thigh, and (3) let go of it to allow it to pivot freely around your left thigh through one complete revolution. (4) As it flies off your left thigh of its own momentum, catch it by letting it fall across the top of your right wrist as you step down and shift your weight to your left leg. (5) Raise your right knee up to waist level as you grip the nunchaku with your right hand. (6) Swing the nunchaku under your right thigh, and let go of it so that it (7) rotates freely around your right thigh through one revolution. (8) As it comes off your right leg, step down and catch the nunchaku by letting it fall across the top of your right wrist.

Twirling Exercise No. 5

(1) Begin with the nunchaku in one hand out to the side. (2) Swing it over to the other side and up toward your opposite shoulder. (3) Flip the free section around the back of your neck, and cross your arms to catch the free section with the other hand as you (4) simultaneously release your original grip. Swing the nunchaku down from behind your neck and (5) out to the side.

1

3

2

4

5

Twirling Exercise No. 6

(1) With the nunchaku at chest level, (2) step forward with your right foot into a right forward stance as you flip the nunchaku over your right shoulder, (3) catching it behind your back with your left hand. (4) Release your right hand grip and swing the nunchaku clear of your back and up to face level to catch it in your right hand. (6) Maintaining both grips, carry the nunchaku to your right side into an over-the-shoulder ready position. (7) Release your left hand grip, strike directly downward, and follow

5

7

Continued

8

through between your legs. (8) Step up with your left foot into a right side stance, catch the nunchaku behind you with your left hand, and (9) releasing your right hand, swing the nunchaku clear of your back and out to the left side. (10) Strike horizontally from left to right, and follow through by (11) swinging it upward around the back of your neck as you pivot into a horse stance. Catch it by crossing your right hand over to your left shoulder. (12) Release your left hand grip, and (13) swing a downward diagonal strike with your left hand, and (14) step back with your right foot into a left forward stance ready position.

10

13

1

12

4

Blocking and Striking

Timing is the key to executing dynamic blocking techniques because the block itself should constitute an offensive option in its own right. Think of the technique of deflecting a front punch for example. The basic block simply pushes the punch out of the way. The dynamic block thrusts a strike to the wrist, damaging the bone at the same time the punch is deflected. Another dynamic blocking technique employs the rope to set up the next move which is often to trap the opponent's limb, and render an armlock, leglock, or wristlock.

Basic striking techniques properly executed can't be improved upon. The use of two nunchaku instead of one introduces the ability to strike more often while sacrificing so much in return, one can only say that double nunchaku are different but not necessarily better. Training with them however will improve your skills considerably, and is highly recommended.

BLOCKING TECHNIQUES

(A) Inside Thrust Block

A punch can be deflected to the inside using the end of one section to thrust a strike to the opponent's wrist.

(B) Downward Thrust Block

Similarly, a punch can be deflected downward while inflicting injury to the wrist at the same time.

A

(C) Trapping Block

A conventional empty-hand type of block using your wrist can be enhanced by trapping the attacker's arm between your wrist and the nunchaku.

(D) Deflection Block

Blows can be deflected by using the nunchaku as you would normally use your wrist or forearm.

(E) Deflection Block with Rope

In preparing for a vise grip trap, use the nunchaku rope to execute the deflection on the opponent's wrist.

C

(F) Elbow Block

Stepping to the outside, an effective block can be applied to the elbow.

(G) Shin Block

When blocking a kick, the opponent's shin is similarly vulnerable.

(H) Sliding Block

A sliding block along the opponent's arm also allows you to control his arm.

F

D

E

G

H

Wrist

Target Areas for Swinging Strikes

Swinging strikes are best applied to areas where the vulnerable anatomical structures are close to the surface. Bony areas of the body, for example, where the bones are fairly fragile, are good targets for swinging strikes. Other areas include the groin and the kidneys.

Temple

Groin

Collarbone

Top of the Head

Knee

Back of the Head

Kidneys

Target Areas for Thrusts

Using the ends of the nunchaku sections to thrust effects precision strikes which are more penetrating than swinging strikes. These kinds of strikes, however, require being in close to your opponent. Thrusts can effectively attack the same targets as swinging strikes, but can also be used to attack parts of the body that swinging strikes cannot, such as the solar plexus which can only be effectively struck with penetrating blows, or pressure points which are extremely precise targets.

Base of the Nose

Top of the Head

Groin

Temple

Throat

Solar Plexus

Ribs

Target Areas for Double Strikes

Striking with both nunchaku at the same time to separate targets is more difficult than it may appear. You may be accustomed to focusing your strikes while looking directly at your target. In this case, you will find yourself trying to decide which of the two targets to focus your eyes on. Try instead not to focus on either one to the exclusion of the other, but to take in both at once. You can do this by using your peripheral vision. It is also advisable to choose targets that are relatively close together.

Both Collarbones

Elbow and Wrist

Collarbone and Head

Forearm and Wrist

Forearm and Knee

High Block, Middle Strike

Simultaneous Block and Strike Techniques

In attempting a simultaneous block and strike, your eyes must take in both targets at once, just as with the double strikes. However, you must also remember that the block is more important than the strike. The block is also the more difficult of the two to execute, requiring sharper judgment. The center of your field of vision should therefore be shifted to favor your blocking target over your striking

High Block, Low Strike

Inside Block, Kidney Strike

target; and your block may even precede your strike by a split second. It isn't necessary that they be precisely simultaneous, only that the strike takes advantage of the natural opening your opponent gives you in delivering his strike. Since this opening only occurs within the short time that he has extended himself into his strike, your strike must be executed within a split second of your block.

Wrist Block, Thrust

Training Exercise
for Blocking and Striking

For this exercise, you need a partner armed with a bo. His bo allows you to execute your blocking and striking with good focus and speed since your target will be the bo in motion and not the person wielding it. This is also a fine training exercise for bo techniques as well. Learn the moves thoroughly so that you can coordinate with your partner to increase the speed and power of the techniques. (1) Stand facing your partner. (2) As your partner attempts an overhead strike, step to the right and deflect the bo by blocking it to the left with a fully focused strike. (3) Your partner then follows with an attempted low strike with the other end of the bo. Step to the left into a left side stance, and block to the right. (4) Your partner comes back to the other side with a strike at your head. Lean back to the right, pivoting into a back stance to execute the block. (5) Your partner pulls back and (6) comes over the top with another overhead strike. Block upward with the nunchaku folded together. (7) Flick a short backhand strike which your partner parries as he pulls back into a cat stance. Then,

5

Continued

(8) as your partner thrusts, block upward with the nunchaku. (9) Pull back, and (10) execute a backhand strike. Your partner parries. (11) Follow with a forehand strike from the other side. (12) Changing your angle of attack slightly, (13) strike from the side. Your partner sidesteps into a back stance to face the blow and execute his block. Then, (14) you sidestep quickly into a left side stance, and

11

12

14

Continued

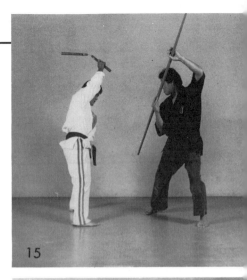

15

(15) attempt a low strike from the back. (16) Your partner dips his bo to protect his rear and executes his block. (17) Catch the nunchaku while your partner brings the bo over to the opposite side. (18&19) When he strikes, execute a side block by shifting the nunchaku into a modified over-the-shoulder position on the right side. (20) Release your left hand, and (21) strike diagonally downward in an inside-out direction at your partner's back. (22) Once again, he dips

17

20

16

18

19

22

99 Continued

23

his bo behind to execute the block. (23) As your partner brings the bo overhead, step back with your left foot into a right forward stance, and (24&25) as he swings the bo down for an overhead strike at your head, (26) block upward. (27) Your partner comes under with the other end to follow up with an attempted low strike. (28) Execute a low block with the nunchaku folded together. (29) Open the nunchaku and (30) strike from the side. Your partner pivots into a side stance to block with the middle of his bo. (31) As your partner leans back to re-

25

28

4

6

27

9

30

31

position his bo for a follow-up, do not break contact, but flip your nunchaku around his bo instead to make his recovery difficult and limit his choices for a quick follow-up. (32) With the nunchaku hung around the bo, your partner's attempted thrust is easily parried. Simply pulling on the nunchaku influences his thrust out to the left side. (33) Your partner pulls back and (34) attempts a side strike. Block this with the nunchaku rope. (35) Reversing to the other side, your partner steps in with his left foot for a low strike to the other side. Step back with your right foot to shift slightly out of range, and (36) strike the bo from behind as it passes in front of you. Strike it with the rope so that the nunchaku begins to flip around it. Then (37) sweep the bo sharply upward to throw it out to the side. Your partner steps with his right into a side stance in order to try to keep control. This completes the exercise. (38) With the exercise at and end, both of you come back to your original positions.

33

36

Fighting Techniques

It takes practice and more practice for nunchaku techniques to become second nature so that you can use them creatively and spontaneously. Here are a series of short technique drills which you should practice with great care, starting slowly until you understand the feeling and intentions of the movements, and then, after the techniques are thoroughly learned, increasing speed.

In these technique drills, your partner will be rendered helpless by your technique and will not be able to protect himself effectively. Therefore, you must take the responsibility for his safety. Be sure to pull your blows long before they even come close enough to be dangerous. Do not try to push your skills to the limit when working with another person. Save that for inanimate targets. With trapping and submission holds, use little force and encourage your partner to go along. If he is slow in doing so, stop the technique.

AGAINST AN ARMED ATTACKER

Sideshift, Trap and Disarm

(1) Both your partner and yourself stand facing each other in ready positions. Your partner, being the attacker, (2) lunges for your midsection with his knife. Shift your body to one side as you raise the nunchaku

overhead. (3) Strike down on your partner's arm with the middle of the nunchaku, and (4) trap his arm in a vise grip. (5) Pivot away from him, and twist the nunchaku to disarm him.

Block and Double Strike

(1) From the ready position, (2) your partner lunges for your midsection with his
knife. Shift your body to one side to
avoid the knife as you deflect your partner's arm with the nunchaku. (3) Step in
to close the distance, and (4&5) deliver a
strike to his midsection with the nunchaku. (6) Step in with the other leg, and
(7) strike to the back of his head.

4

5

7

Sidestep and Strike

(1) As your partner prepares for a downward stab, grip the nunchaku at both ends. (2) Your partner brings the knife downward toward

your chest. Step to one side to avoid his stab, and (3&4) flick the nunchaku with an underhand motion to (5) strike the side of his head.

Sideshift, Block, Pivot, Trap and Disarm

(1) From the ready position, (2) your partner steps in with a stab at your midsection, swinging from the outside inward. Open the nunchaku, and (3) step in as you block his weapon with the rope of the nunchaku. (4) Pivot in toward his body with your back as you maintain your block on his weapon hand to hold it away from you. Then, (5&6) trap his weapon arm by the wrist in a vise grip with the nunchaku, and (7) twist to disarm him.

5

Sidestep and Inside Strike

(1) From the ready position, your partner (2) lunges with the point of his knife. Sidestep out of the way as you raise the nunchaku over your head, and in one

smooth motion, (3-6) swing the nunchaku in a diagonal from the outside inward to strike the side of his head from his blind side.

Sidestep and Outside Strike

(1) From the ready position, your partner (2) lunges for your midsection with the point of his knife. As you sidestep out of the way, bring your nunchaku into an over-the-shoulder ready position on your right side.

In one smooth motion, (4&5) release your left hand grip, and strike down through an inside-out diagonal path, approaching from his blind side, to strike to the back of his head.

Sidestep and Strike

(1) From your ready position with the nunchaku behind you, prepare for your partner's attack. The advantage of having the nunchaku behind you is that you are able to strike faster. If the nunchaku was forward to begin with, you would first have to bring it into striking position. This betrays your angle

of attack. With the nuncha-ku behind you, you can strike out from either side without warning. Your part-ner attempts a stab. (2) Shift out of range of his stab, and (3) swinging from the left side, (4&5) strike with the nunchaku to the back of his head from his blind side.

Backshift and Overhead Strike

(1) As your partner prepares to stab, (2) raise the nunchaku overhead. This takes it out of his immediate visual range. (3) Shift out of range as he extends the knife and (4&5) strike down on the top

of his head. Since the nunchaku has a longer reach than a knife, moving just outside your opponent's range still keeps him within your range for a counterattack.

High Block and Low Strike

(1) From the ready position, your partner (2) attempts an overhead strike with his bo. Block upward with the rope of the nunchaku, as you (3) shift forward to close the distance, forcing the bo up-

ward at an angle. (4) Quickly release your left hand grip, and swing the nunchaku out to the side and then down in a circular path to (5) strike to the shin.

Double Block and Overhead Strike

(1) From the ready position, your partner (2) attempts a strike at your head with the bo. Execute an outside block with one section of the nunchaku while securing the other section with the other hand. (3) Your partner follows with another attempt with the other end of the bo. (4) Execute an inside block with the same section. Then (5) immediately take the offense by (6) coming over the top with (7) a strike to the top of his head.

Rope Block, Leg Block and Strike

(1) From the ready position, your partner (2) moves foward, (3) dropping his shoulders lower, indicating his intention to deliver a low strike. (4) As he brings his nunchaku into motion, you do the same, to (5) meet his weapon with your own, striking the rope of his nunchaku, causing his weapon to flip out of control. Take care to raise your leg to avoid his nunchaku. (6) Block his arm outward with your leg, and (7) raising your nunchaku overhead, (8) finish him by striking down on the back of his head.

Double Side Block and Strike

(1) From the ready position, (2) your partner prepares to strike. Bring the nunchaku into a blocking position. (3) As he strikes to your side, shift the nunchaku back into an over-the-shoulder position to block. (4-7) Your partner strikes again to the side. Block again by shifting the nunchaku back to protect your side. Then (8) counter immediately by striking to his elbow joint.

Rope Block, Strike and Disarm

(1) From the ready position, (2) your partner attempts a swipe at your midsection. Shift back just barely out of range to let his weapon go by. (3) He follows immediately by attempting a back-

hand swing for your head. (4)
As his nunchaku comes up,
strike the rope to cause his
nunchaku to flip. Then (5)
grab the striking section of
his nunchaku with your free

131 Continued

hand, (6) pull him closer, and (7-9) strike down on the side of his head to weaken his grip on his weapon. (10) At

that instant, (11) strike to the other side of his head with his own weapon.

Deflection Block and Double Strike

(1) From the ready position, your partner faces you armed with a bo. (2) He begins to move in, swinging the bo back in preparation for an overhead strike. (3) As he strikes down toward you, step out to one side, and (4) deflect the bo outward with

one section of the nunchaku. (5) Follow up by striking
his arm with the other section, then (6) swipe across
his midsection, neutralizing
his ability to follow up. (7)
Step in close, and (8) strike
down across the back of his
head.

Rope Block and Double Strike

(1) From the ready position, you face your partner who is also armed with a nunchaku. (2) As he steps forward with an overhead strike, (3) bring your nunchaku in motion to (4) strike his weapon as it comes toward you. Strike his weapon exactly on the rope. This will neutralize his attemped blow, causing him to (5) lose control of it momentarily. (6&7) Before he can recover, step in and immediately swipe across his midsection, then (8-10) come over the top to finish him with a strike to the back of his head.

7

AGAINST AN UNARMED ATTACKER

Trap and Submission

(1) From the ready position, your partner (2) moves in to attempt a front punch. (3) Shift back out of range, and as he extends his fist, trap his wrist in a vise grip with the nunchaku. (4) Pull his arm down using the nuncha-

ku hold. (5) Bringing your other hand from behind his legs, switch the nunchaku to the other hand, (6) tying up your partner in a helpless position, and neutralizing his offensive capacity.

Escape, Trap and Throw

(1&2) Your partner grabs you by the lapels. (3) Place the nunchaku across the tops of his wrists, trapping his hands against your chest.

Bending forward, drop to one knee, forcing your partner to the ground. Then, by (4) twisting your body, throw him over to one side.

Headlock, Throw
and Stranglehold Submission

(1) As you face your partner in the ready position, hold the folded nunchaku in one hand. (2) Your partner grabs you by the belt to hold you in position as he prepares to strike with the other hand. (3) Bring the nunchaku up, (4) raising it overhead as your partner begins his punch. (5) As he punches, bring the nunchaku down on the back of his neck, pulling him toward you, and stopping his technique. (6) Step out to the side as you twist the nunchaku to pinch your partner's neck in a vise grip. (7) Pull him to the ground, and apply a stranglehold with the nunchaku.

Downward Block, Trap, and Throw

(1) From your ready position, (2) your partner steps in to attempt a front punch. As he steps in, raise the nunchaku overhead. (3) When he extends his punch, lean back out of range, and bring the nunchaku down on his wrist to deflect the punch. Then, (5-7) wrap the nunchaku around his wrist to (8) trap his wrist in a vise grip, and (9) throw him to the ground.

Double Block and Trap

(1) From the ready position, (2) your partner steps in for a front punch. (3) As he extends his arm, sideshift to avoid the strike, and execute an inside block with one section of the nunchaku. (4) Keeping contact with his arm, force it out and down in a circular motion, then (5) completing the circle, swing it over to the other side. (6) Your partner follows with a reverse punch. Block it with the middle of the nunchaku, (7) trap his wrist in a vise grip, and (8) twist to make him submit.

2

4

5

7

8

Headlock and Throw

(1) Your partner grabs you in a bearhug from behind. (2) Open the nunchaku as you raise it above your head and (3) reach back to trap your partner's head in a headlock with the nunchaku. Then, (4) pull him around to your side as you block his legs with yours, and (5) throw him to the ground.

5

Bearhug Escape, Armlock, and Throw

(1) Your partner grabs you from behind in a bearhug, also pinning your upper arms to the sides of your body. (2&3) Bring the nunchaku up and place it under your partner's grip, between his clasped hands and your body. (4) Using the leverage of the nunchaku, break his grip, and trap one of his arms. (5) Pivot out, and execute an armlock with the nunchaku (6) to throw your partner to the ground.

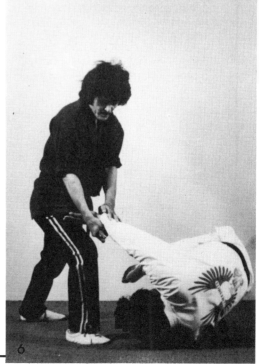

Rear Shoulder Grab Escape
and Outside Armbar Submission

(1) Your partner, in preparation for an assault, grabs you by your shoulder. (2&3) Turn to spot his position, then pivot out to one side, raising your arm up over his head. (4) Bring your arm down, over his arm, breaking his grip on your shoulder. (5) Circle your arm under his, and at the same time, place the nunchaku over his elbow joint, gripping the other end of the nunchaku with your other hand, and forming a fulcrum for an armbar. (7) Force your opponent to the ground by pushing down while keeping his arm trapped in the armbar.

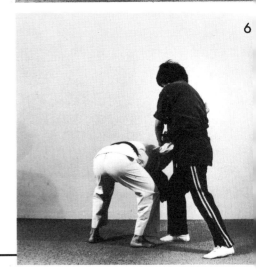

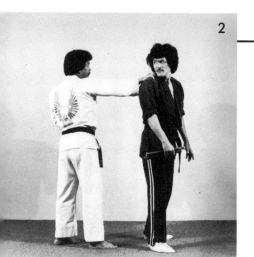

Rear Shoulder Grab Escape and Inside Armbar Submission

(1) Your partner grabs you by the shoulder. (2) First, turn to spot him, then (3) pivot to the outside, but bring the nunchaku up on the inside over his arm. (4) Apply an armbar, and by pushing down, (5) force him to the ground.

Applications

Study these scenarios in which the nunchaku is used in self-defense, and consider those moments when the situation is turned in the defender's favor. What did he do to cause this? Often, it is obvious—trapping the attacker's hand, using his block as a striking technique and so forth. Other times, however, it is subtle—a matter of footwork, angling the body in a certain way, shifting to a strategically advantageous position.

Notice that although every situation is different, the action follows certain discernable phases: attack, defend, counterattack. Upon the initial move by the attacker, the defender blocks, or otherwise neutralizes the strike, then shifts to the inside or outside of the attacker's line of attack for the final step which is to land a strike of his own. Shifting to the outside is safer, but leaves the defender fewer vulnerable targets. Shifting to the inside gives the defender access to the front of the attacker's body, but puts him in a position to which the attacker can more easily adjust.

Self-Defense Application No. 1

(1) As the defender steps out of his car, he is faced with an assailant. (2) The attacker comes at the defender with an overhead strike. The defender leans back out of range, and cocks his leg. (3) To deliver a front kick to the attacker's midsection, and (4) following through to send the attacker reeling back, the defender (5) retrieves the nunchaku he had hidden in his sock. (6) The defender brings the nunchaku back, (7) cocks it with his other hand as the attacker comes forward again, and (8) snaps a strike to the attacker's face. (9) The attacker falls back on the hood of the car stunned, and the defender (10) finishes with a strike to the attacker's midsection.

7

8

Self-Defense Application No. 2

(1) An assailant approaches the defender from behind as he is closing the trunk of his car. (2&3) The attacker grabs the defender by the shoulder and turns him around to deliver a strike to his face. The defender quickly reaches behind and pulls his nunchaku from his back pocket. (4) He opens it just in time to (5) bring it down as the attacker swings for his face, (6) catching the attacker's wrist in a vise grip, and gaining control. (7) The defender then brings his feet together as he twists the nunchaku to tighten his grip on the attacker's wrist. (8) The defender steps forward, and, using his body momentum, (9) extends his leg, and throws the attacker. (10) Once the attacker is on the ground, the defender finishes with a final strike.

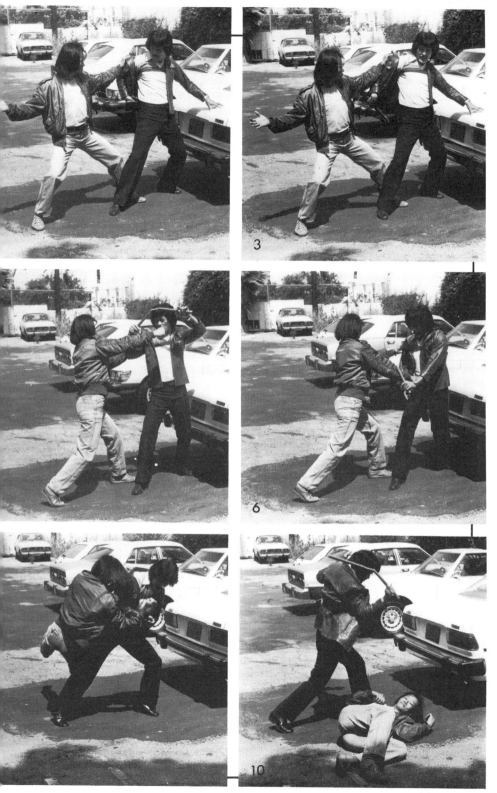

Self-Defense Application No. 3

(1) Getting out of his new car, the defender comes face to face with an attacker preparing to attack him with a chain. (2) The defender reaches for his nunchaku, and (3) pulls it out just as the attacker cocks his arm to swing. (4) The attacker goes for the defender's head, but misses as the defender ducks under the attempted blow. (5) The defender shifts to one side, and (6) raises the nunchaku overhead, (7) striking down on the attacker's weapon arm and disabling it temporarily. (8) The attacker, stunned by the blow to his arm, falls back against the car. (9) The defender moves in, strikes to the throat, and then (10) executes a powerful downward blow to the midsection with both ends of the nunchaku.

163

Self-Defense Application No. 4

(1) The defender is backed against his car as the attacker approaches. (2) The attacker attempts a front kick, and the defender, pulling his nunchaku from behind, (3) blocks the kick, and immediately traps the attacker's ankle in a vise grip with the nunchaku. (4) The defender turns the attacker's leg using the nunchaku so that, to avoid further injury, the attacker (5) must fall to the ground. (6) The defender releases his grip on the attacker's ankle, (7) steps around to his side, and (8) finishes him with a strike to the groin.

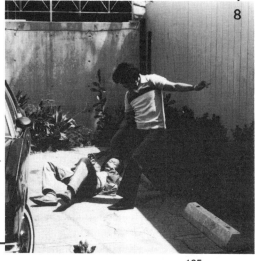

Self-Defense Application No. 5

(1) Unknown to the two attackers who confront him, the single defender has a nunchaku tucked into his back pocket. (2) Both attackers grab the defender by the collar at the same time. (3) Pulling the nunchaku from

behind, the defender raises it overhead, (4) opens it as he brings it down, to (5) trap the hands of both attackers in a vise grip. (6) He then twists the nunchaku to break their grip on his collar,

Continued

(7) releases the vise grip, and (8) strikes one attacker to the head, (9) knocking him to the ground. (10) The defender then turns to the other attacker, cocking back the nunchaku. (11) He

strikes him in the head to (12) send him falling to the ground. As he is going down, the defender comes back the other way to finish with a strike to the lower back.

Self-Defense Application No. 6

(1) The defender faces two attackers. One of them grabs the defender by the shoulder. (2) The defender moves his arm under the attacker's arm and (3) brings the end of the nunchaku over the top of his forearm, then, placing his other hand under the arm, traps it, and gains control of the first attacker. (4) The second attacker attempts a reverse front punch, and the defender blocks the attempt by throwing the other attacker's arm in the way, deflecting the blow. (5) With both attackers in each other's way and arms crossed, neither is able to follow up effectively. (6) The defender then uses this to his advantage by striking to the midsection of the second attacker, (7) turning swiftly, and (8) striking to the midsection of the first attacker, then (9&10) finishing them both with a swipe across their heads in one stroke.

Self-Defense Application No. 7

(1) As the defender steps out of his car, he is confronted by an attacker who holds a knife in one hand. (2) As the attacker raises his knife, the defender raises his nunchaku, gripping it with both hands. (3) The defender opens the nunchaku as the attacker moves forward with the knife. (4) The attacker attempts a lunge with the point of the knife. The defender shifts his body to one side, and uses the open nunchaku to deflect the strike to the other side. (5) Moving quickly, the defender wraps the nunchaku around the attacker's wrist, pinching and trapping his weapon hand. (6) With the attacker's weapon hand in a vise grip, the defender (7) yanks it forcefully over to the other side as he steps in, weakening the attacker's grip on the knife and moving himself closer for a

7

Continued

counterattack. (8) The defender strikes the attacker with one end of the nuncha-ku, (9) steps back quickly while the attacker is still stunned, and (10&11) strikes the attacker's knife hand, disarming him. (12) The defender steps back even farther, and (13&14) delivers a finishing blow to the side of the attacker's head.

12

Self-Defense Application No. 8

(1) The defender is approached by two attackers. One is armed with a short stick, and the other wields a chain. The defender carries two nunchaku, one in each hand. Both attackers converge on the defender. (2) The attacker with the chain makes the first move, throwing the end toward the defender's head. The defender deals with that by simply taking a step forward, (3) stepping between the attackers and out of their lines of convergence. The end of the chain misses to one side while the length of chain falls harmlessly over the defender's outstretched arm. At the same time, the other attacker with the short stick, seeing the defender move from directly in front of him to his side, attempts a low side strike. The defender deflects it with his other nunchaku. (4) With the chain's momentum spent, the defender turns his attention to the man with the stick who is capable of recovering faster and striking again. (5) Another low side strike with the stick is attempted; and the defender blocks that easily as well. (6) Stepping even further between the armed men and away from their effective striking angles, the defender turns to the chain opponent, and (7) puts him away with a strike to the head, pivoting at the same time to (8) face the same direction as the attackers, and standing side by side with them. (9) His opponents are now helpless to strike effectively due to their positions relative to the defender, whereas the defender's pivoting momentum allows him to deliver a strike to the back of the head of the stick opponent.

Self-Defense Application No. 9

(1) Faced with two attackers about the same distance away, the defender decides to strike first by (2) stepping closer to one opponent and farther away from the other. This enables him to deal with them one at a time. (3)

He strikes the closer of the two across the jaw, and (4) as he retreats from the conflict, the defender turns to face the second whom he (5) dispatches with a strike to the side of the head.

Self-Defense Application No. 10

(1) Faced with two attackers, the defender stands his ground with the nunchaku behind his back. (2) As the attackers prepare to launch their assault, the defender raises his nunchaku overhead. (3) The first attacker lunges with a punch, and the defender deflects his blow with the nunchaku. (4) Pivoting completely around, the defender turns to face the second man who (5) throws a punch toward the defender's face. The defender deflects the blow upward, (6) swings back to strike the first attacker in the lower back, (7) shifts his weight back then (8) steps out to the side. (9) He pivots away from the second attacker, and (10) strikes with a backhand motion to the attacker's face.

Self-Defense Application No. 11

(1) The attacker has the defender in a headlock, but the defender reacts immediately by bringing the nunchaku out to one side of the attacker's body, (2) hooking his leg, and trapping it so he can't step back. Then, (3) stepping around his leg, the defender moves his body around behind the attacker who still tries to maintain the headlock. The turned position of the defender's body, however, has weakened the headlock. (4) As the defender continues to turn, he breaks the headlock, and (5) takes advantage of the attacker's locked arm

5

Continued

position to (6-9) strike down on the shoulder joint, dislocating the shoulder. (10) Holding the attacker's locked arm in place, the defender gains control of the situation.

Self-Defense Application No. 12

The defender (1) is back against a fence, and is confronted by an attacker. The attacker (2) throws a punch for the defender's face, and the defender shifts to one side, avoiding the blow. The defender (3) deflects the attacker's arm with the nunchaku to the outside. The attacker (4) attemps to come around the block with the other fist, but the defender also blocks that attempt. The defender (5) pulls back the nunchaku, and (6) captures the defender's striking arm by wrapping the nunchaku around it. (7) He then applies an armlock, forcing the attacker down to a vulnerable position, and (8) finishes him off with a knee strike to the side of the head.

5

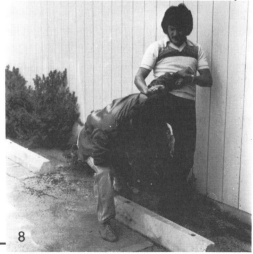

8

Self-Defense Application No. 13

(1) The attacker grabs the defender by the throat with both hands to choke him. (2) The defender brings both his hands up between the attacker's arms, (3) opens the nunchaku, gripping both nunchaku sections in the middle. (4) Catching the attacker's arms with the ends of the sections, the defender brings the nunchaku down forcefully, causing the attacker to release his grip. (5) The defender pushes the attacker back by thrusting to his throat, and (6) the attacker falls back off balance.

189

Self-Defense Application No. 14

The defender (1) is grabbed by the attacker who prepares to strike him with a punch. The defender (2) opens the nunchaku, and (3) as the attacker fires his punch, the defender (4) deflects it and wraps the nunchaku around his wrists. The defender then (5) pulls the attacker's punching hand over his grabbing hand, thus trapping both hands together with the nunchaku. The defender (6) pushes the attacker back by controlling both his hands. (7) He pulls down hard to throw the attacker's hands apart, then (8) strikes him to the throat with the nunchaku.

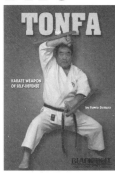

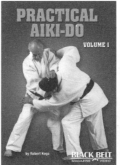
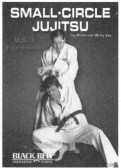